# The Joy

# OF Drawing

### Exploring the Beauty of Artistic Expression

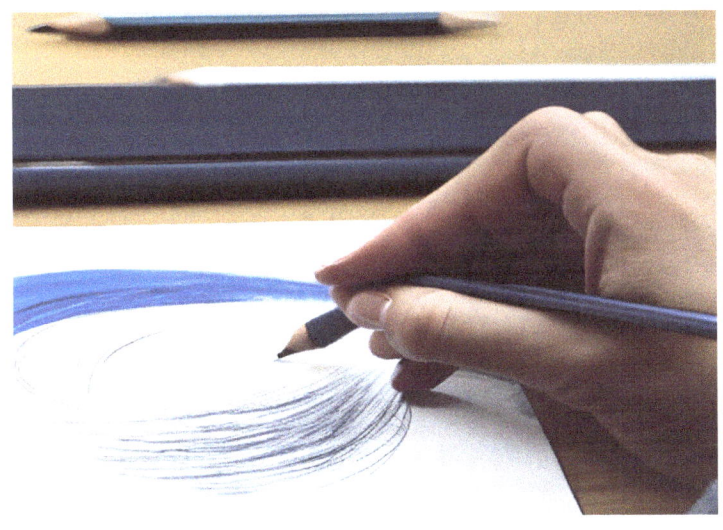

# UNDERSTANDING BASIC SHAPES AND FORMS ........28

# Introduction

Drawing is an ageless art form that enables us to express our creative potential and record the world around us in a manner that is singular and reflective of our own experiences. This guide is intended to help you engage on a journey of discovery and self-expression via the medium of drawing, whether you are an amateur artist looking to explore your artistic abilities or an established artist looking to better your skills. It may be used by either novice or expert artists.

Your artistic endeavors might benefit immensely from "Getting Started with Drawing," which provides a rock-solid basis on which to build. To get started on your path as an artist, let's talk about the tools and supplies that you absolutely need to have. We are going to discuss the instruments, such as sketchbooks and pencils, as well as erasers and sharpeners that will become your reliable companions as you embark on your journey into the world of drawing.

It is vital for each artist to have a fundamental understanding of drawing techniques and principles. In the first chapter, we are going to investigate the fundamental ideas that govern the art of drawing. You will acquire a thorough understanding of these essential principles, which will establish the framework for your artistic progress. These important concepts range from line work and shading to composition and perspective.

We'll be taking a more in-depth look at pencils and graphite techniques, investigating the wide variety of effects that can be achieved using these mediums. After that, we will delve into the world of charcoal and investigate its distinctive characteristics as well as the effects it has on the surrounding air. We will discuss how to make the most of the precision and texture that can be achieved through the use of pen and ink in your drawings. In addition, we will explore the kaleidoscopic possibilities offered by colored pencils as well as the mellow, blended results offered by pastels.

When it comes to producing realistic drawings, the ability to recognize and faithfully reproduce even the most fundamental shapes and forms is absolutely necessary. We will help you develop your observation abilities and show you how to convert what you see onto writing by providing you with direction and leading you through activities. In addition to this, we will investigate drawing fundamental three-dimensional forms and strategies for creating shading that gives the illusion of depth and dimension.

You will finish this course with a firm foundation in drawing skills, an understanding of numerous drawing tools, and the capacity to make drawings that are accurate representations of the world around you. This guide will provide you with the knowledge and skills necessary to go on an artistic journey that is both rewarding and successful, regardless of whether your objective is to create representations that are realistic or to express your creativity via artworks that are stylized. As a result, get all of your supplies together, organize your drawing space, and get ready to enter the fascinating world of drawing together.

# Getting started with drawing

Taking your first steps in drawing may be a journey that is both exciting and gratifying.

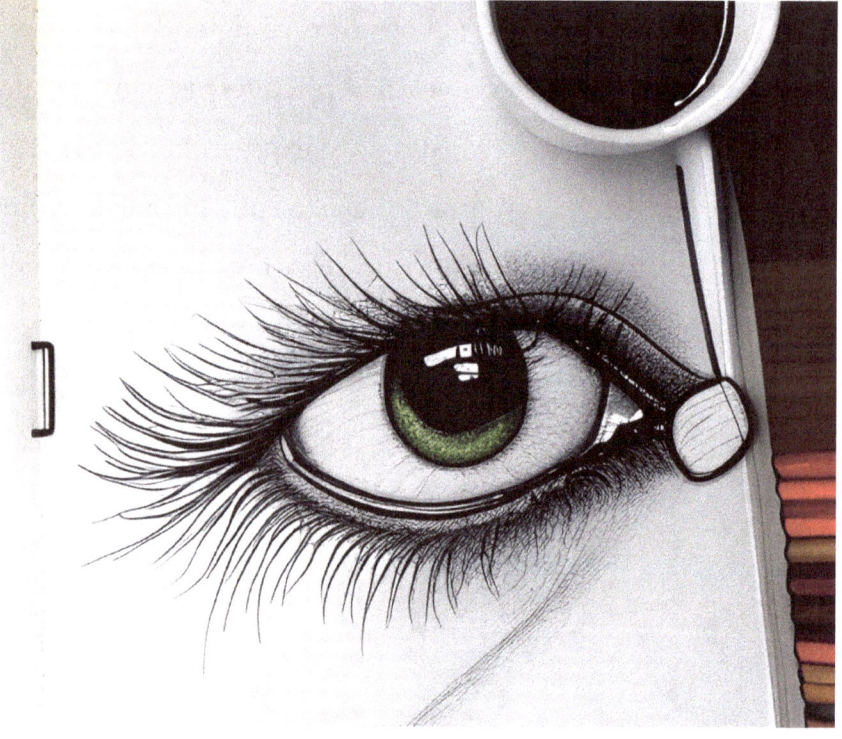

The following are some steps that will assist you in getting started:

## Gatherings the necessary materials:

## Paper:

To get started, grab a drawing pad or sketchbook. Pick a size that is appropriate for you based on your preferences.

## Pencils:

Obtain a number of graphite pencils in varying degrees of hardness, such as HB, 2B, 4B, and 6B. These distinct grades come in a wide range of colors and varying degrees of brittleness.

## Erasers:

Have both a kneaded eraser and a vinyl eraser on hand so that you can lift graphite and erase more precisely, respectively.

## Sharpeners:

Purchase a sharpener that is designed for graphite pencils, and if possible, choose one that has a variety of different sized holes.

## The use of colored pencils

If you are an artist or have an interest in art and drawing, you really need to have colored pencils in your home. These are wonderful since you can put them to a variety of uses, including the following:

- Produce works of art that are stunning and vibrant;
- Make coloring pages out of them with their help;

- Drawing, be it a sketch or a doodle.
- You've just created a watercolor painting by combining the paint with some water.

There are numerous different packs on the market, each containing a unique quantity of colored pencils. When it comes to colored pencils, you won't have much success if you try to mix colors, so investing in a large case is your best bet.

## Eraser

Despite the fact that I believe we should leave our faults in our drawings and correct them in another illustration, there are times when erasers are still required due to the nature of the task.

If you're just doodling or sketching for pleasure, I wouldn't bother bringing an eraser with you. Instead, you should just give yourself permission to make as many mistakes as you like.

This is a wonderful method for remembering your errors, so that you can learn from them and perform the same actions in a different manner the following time.

If you keep an eraser close by, you will feel forced to make immaculate drawings in which there is not a single line that is out of place. It's quite fine to make a mess sometimes; in fact, you should encourage it.

However, an eraser is necessary for specific types of work. For very simple drawings and for making tiny adjustments, you can use the white eraser that comes with your pencil.

It is always a smart alternative to have on hand, even if you don't have anything else at home. However, a word of caution: these are quite tough, and it is well-known that using them to erase large portions of paper will actually destroy the paper.

## Sketchbook

It is essential for any artist to keep a sketchbook. Not just to draw on it, but also to jot down ideas and other essential notes, it may be used for both. You are not required to make use of it each and every single day. It is not necessary for the location to be neat and well-organized either.

When I think of a sketchbook, I usually think of it as a place to draw, but I also think of it as a journal. Your ideas, your thoughts, and the things you've learnt, etc. These may or may not have anything to do with art. It is completely up to you!

## Paper Pad

Sketchbooks are for jotting down new experiences, developing new skills, and performing warm-up exercises. Additionally, you can use them to create thumbnails of various compositions and concepts for a new illustration.

When you are ready to sketch the final version, however, you will need a high-quality canvas that is constructed from the appropriate paper.

## Inking Pens

You'll probably enjoy working with ink pens if you're someone who enjoys creating line art. There is a wide variety of tip sizes and shapes, ranging from fine tips for creating accurate lines to brush tips for producing lines with greater versatility.

When working with mediums that are less forgiving, such as pencils, one of the best ways to practice is to use pens and markers. Although it will be more difficult to delete mistakes made here, it will still be possible to cover them up.

On the other hand, your motions remind me of the ones you do when you're writing with a pencil.

## Paint Made with Watercolors

A popular media of days is watercolor. Because the paint is diluted with water, you do not require any extra specialized product in order to mix it or clean it up.

The paintings have an air of calm and serenity about them thanks to the watery consistency of the paint.

It's not as simple as it seems, despite the fact that it's a very pleasurable medium. It is necessary to go through a process of trial and error, attend perhaps a few tutorials, and put in a lot of practice. It is not as simple as it may appear to maintain a balance between the amount of color and its intensity.

Therefore, it is acceptable to start with less expensive materials when beginning anything new that you are unsure whether or not you will continue with. When compared to the other mediums we've discussed, watercolor painting is typically more expensive.

## Art Canvas

Drawing and painting can be done on a wide variety of surfaces. Paper is the most accessible medium, and a good place to begin because it enables even the most basic printer paper to be transformed into something stunning. Although it's not ideal, it's not impossible either!

If you wish to paint, though, it could be intriguing for you to try painting on an art canvas at some point in the future. This canvas has more texture to work with, and it has a greater potential to last longer.

Because it is composed of a different substance, there is no need for you to worry about accidentally destroying it by using wet products like acrylics; this is not the case.

The use of canvas, on the other hand, may inspire more anxiety due to the fact that it behaves significantly differently and it is not as simple to correct errors when they occur.

## Drawing Glove

When sketching, drawing gloves are almost always used in conjunction with a drawing tablet. These days, a drawing glove is included with the majority of drawing tablets so that users can draw without making smudges.

On the other hand, I've discovered that these can be quite helpful when painting or drawing in the traditional manner. As you sketch, your hand will move across the canvas in various places.

This same hand will, at some point or another, come into contact with the graphite, paint, charcoal, or any other substance that you are working with.

When anything like that occurs, you run the risk of smudging the paper with your hand. Even when you have a lot of experience, it is inevitable that you will make mistakes.

## Setting up a dedicated workspace:

- Invest in a desk lamp or look for a room that has adequate lighting, such as one that gets plenty of natural light.
- Make sure you have a firm table or easel to work on, as well as a chair that is comfortable for you to sit in.
- Maintain your materials in an organized fashion that is well within your reach and is simple to access.
- It is important to have a clutter-free environment in which to sketch so that you can concentrate on the task at hand.

## Understanding basic drawing techniques and concepts:

Drawing contours requires practice drawing the outlines of items while paying attention to the forms and contours of those objects.

### Shading:

You may give your drawings more depth and character by experimenting with different shading techniques. Beginning with basic hatching (lines that are parallel to one another) and cross-hatching (lines that overlap one another).

## Value:

Gain an understanding of the value notion, which relates to the gradation of lightness to darkness that exists in a painting. Exercises should be done to achieve varied values by manipulating the amount of pressure that is applied to the pencil.

## Proportions:

When creating your drawings, make sure to give careful consideration to the relative sizes of the various elements. To guarantee that your work is accurate, use straightforward methods such as measuring or following the lead of your pencil.

Learn the fundamentals of one-point and two-point perspective to provide the impression of depth and three-dimensional space in your drawings using the technique of perspective.

# Practice regularly:

- Regularly allot time in your schedule specifically for drawing. Regular practice is absolutely necessary if you want to improve your talents.

- Get your feet wet with uncomplicated things and work your way up to more difficult topics as your comfort level increases.

- Explore a variety of topics, approaches, and modes of expression through the process of experimentation in order to hone your artistic sensibilities and identify your personal inclinations.

## Seek inspiration and guidance:

- Try finding ideas for your artwork in art books, internet galleries, museums, or even the natural world.

- Joining art forums or taking part in drawing challenges are great ways to meet other creative people and get feedback on your work.

- You might want to think about enrolling in art lessons, either in person or online, so that you can gain knowledge from seasoned teachers and receive organized direction.

- Always keep in mind that the best way to improve your drawing skills is to sketch on a regular basis and be willing to try out new things. Have fun with it, be patient with yourself, and don't be scared to learn from your mistakes. Enjoy the process. Happy sketching!

# Easy tips to start drawing

### Have faith that you can reach your goal.

Beginning to draw is an activity that may be incredibly nerve-wracking, particularly if you are under the impression that you are unable to draw. There are a surprising number of people who are under the impression that they are unable to draw. This is a very limiting belief that one has about themselves.

If you have the mindset that you cannot accomplish something, then you will never be able to. However, the fact of the matter is that anyone can draw.

It's true that some people are born with the intrinsic capacity to depict form and shape in a highly expressive or realistic way. But not everyone has this talent. The fact that you do not (yet) possess the same degree of ability does not mean that you will never be able to reach that level!

### Don't stress out about being flawless!

Make an effort to concentrate on the act of drawing. Perfectionism is the enemy of creativity and is frequently the reason why individuals stop painting altogether or never begin to draw in the first place.

The reality is that the ability to draw is comparable to any other skill. If you want to learn how to start drawing, you need to be determined and practice sketching over and over again until you get it right. Take it easy on yourself and make sure you practice every day.

## Learning to see is at the heart of drawing.

Learning to draw is not so much about "learning to draw" as it is about learning to SEE, and this is what makes the concept of learning to draw such an exciting one. In other words, we need to start actually looking at our topic with new eyes and a different perspective.

Once you begin to look at things as if you have never seen them before, you can then begin translating what you see into a drawing, which is when the magic starts to happen.

## Make your selection from the available topics.

You have an almost limitless variety of options available to you for the subject matter of your drawing. You can draw from anything in your thoughts or from something that exists in the physical world. You also do not need to limit yourself to drawing traditional subjects; go ahead and get started on a drawing of a giraffe or a unicorn if you like! A great number of famous artists got their start by merely creating cartoon figures.

# Exploring Different Drawing Tools

Discovering your chosen medium and opening up new creative avenues are both possible outcomes of experimenting with a variety of drawing tools.

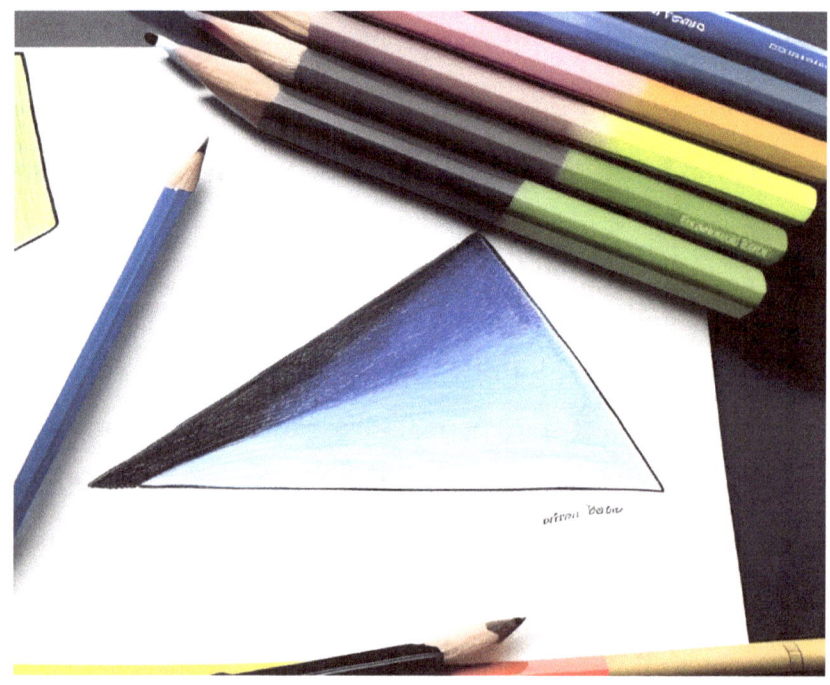

The following is a rundown of several common drawing tools and the distinctive effects that they produce.

# Pencils and graphite techniques:

## Graphite pencils:

These are the most typical instruments used for drawing. They are available in a variety of grades, from hard (which is lighter) to soft (which is darker). By experimenting with different pressure settings and stacking techniques, you may produce a wide range of tones and textures.

## Sticks made of graphite:

These are thicker variants of graphite, which enable the use of wider strokes and more subtle shading. They are wonderful for covering larger areas in a shorter amount of time.

## Mechanical pencils:

These are ideal for tasks that requires precision and convenience. They come with leads that can be swapped out, which guarantees a continuously pointed end.

# Charcoal and its unique effects:

### Vine charcoal:

The ability to smear and mix is made simple with this pliable and lightweight charcoal. It works quite well for doing sketches with a lot of expression and gesturing.

### Charcoal that has been compressed:

It can take the form of a stick or a pencil and produces lines that are more dense and black. It can be helpful in achieving rich values and textures in your artwork.

### Charcoal pencils:

These have the portability of a pencil and the expressive potential of charcoal in one convenient package. They make it possible to create controlled lines as well as smearing effects.

# Pen and ink for precision and texture:

### Drawing pens:

These pens are available in a range of sizes and feature a variety of tips, such as pointed fine liners and broad brush points. They offer lines that are uniform and accurate, making them appropriate for detailed drawings.

### Dip pens:

These need dipping a metal nib into ink. They come in a variety of line widths and allow the user to produce expressive strokes by adjusting the amount of pressure they apply.

### Washes of ink:

When ink is diluted with water, intriguing grayscale values and textural effects can be produced. It enables the creation of regulated lines in addition to larger washes.

# Colored pencils and their vibrant possibilities:

### Pencils of various colors:

They are available in a plethora of colors and provide both control and precision in use. The techniques of layering and blending can be used to create effects that are vivid and have smooth gradients.

### Colored pencils for watercolor:

These pencils can be utilized in the same manner as conventional colored pencils, but they also have the added benefit of transforming into watercolors when activated with water. Blending and the creation of washes are both possible with them.

# Pastels and their soft, blended effects:

## Soft pastels:

Powdered pigment is used in their creation, and a binder is used to keep everything together. They are applied straight to the paper, which results in colors that are incredibly brilliant and rich. They are able to be mixed together and stacked to create a dreamy and soft look.

## Oil pastels:

These are very much like soft pastels, except they are bound together with oil instead of chalk, which gives them a creamy consistency. They can be blended with fingers or with a tool specifically designed for that purpose, and the resulting layers can be rather opaque and thick.

Experimenting with these tools will help you gain a better understanding of their distinctive characteristics and will enable you to identify the effects that appeal to you the most. Keep in mind that you may get the most out of any medium by practicing and experimenting with a variety of various techniques.

# Understanding basic shapes and forms

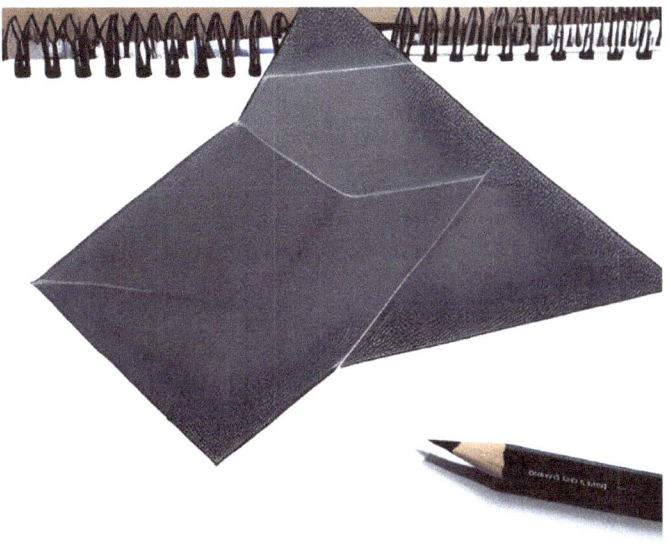

It doesn't matter if you're a novice or a seasoned professional; having a solid grasp of fundamental forms and shapes is an absolutely necessary talent for any artist. Mastering these ideas is essential if one wishes to produce drawings that are both realistic and engaging because they are the fundamental components of any visual art. In this tutorial, we will discuss the fundamental ideas of shape and form, and we will also offer you with some pointers and approaches that you can use to incorporate these ideas into your artwork. So let's get started!

# Importance of observation and perception:

## Observation:

It is of the utmost importance that you cultivate your capacity to notice and evaluate the world around you. It is important to take note of the forms, proportions, and connections between the various things.

## Perception:

You can learn to detect the fundamental geometric features that make up objects by training your eyes to look past the labels on things. Having this ability will allow you to break down complicated topics into their fundamental components.

### Try to Locate the Form

The value that is currently associated with the subject is what conveys the form of the subject to the observer. The viewer is given information about the form of the subject based on the relationships between those values.

The majority of things will have clearly delineated areas of value that can be pinpointed.

## Keep an eye out for the Textures.

In a drawing or painting, the relationships of value are used to communicate texture, just as they are used to communicate shape. The directional marks, regardless of whether they were produced with a pencil or a brush, are an important component as well.

The directional marks and value relationships work together to create the impression of texture in the artwork.

## Keep an Eye Out for the Colors

When creating an observational drawing or painting, the color is, of course, an important aspect that needs to be paid particular attention to. The observation itself is not always where the challenge lies when it comes to applying color; rather, the challenge lies in the mixing of the colors that have been noticed.

A little bit of experience and familiarity with the medium is required to successfully mix colors. Different mediums demand different mixing processes. It is not possible to blend oil paintings in the same way that one might blend colored pencils, for instance.

Even while it may seem like the most crucial thing in the world to match the color as precisely as possible, the value of the color that is applied is actually a more important element. It is possible to entirely change the colors, but as long as the value remains the same, the subject will still be communicated.

## The Central Idea

Have you picked up on a common thread? If you're perceptive, you've undoubtedly observed that six of the seven aspects of art are represented by the objects that are listed below.

- Line
- Shape
- Form
- Value
- Texture
- Color

"Space," which is communicated by a range of characteristics including positioning, value, color, intricacy, overlapping, and size, is the only component that is lacking.

Knowing what exactly to look for is the most important step in the "looking" process. When we make an observational drawing or painting, we are communicating the subject through the various components of the artwork that we produce.

# Drawing basic geometric shapes:

## Circle:

Drawing circles of varying diameters is a good drawing exercise. Begin with rough, quick sketches, then progressively get more detailed with them.

## Square:

Create squares with lines that are straight and even and sides that are the same length. It's important to pay attention to both the angles and the proportions.

## Triangle:

Explore a variety of triangles, such as equilateral, isosceles, and scalene triangles, through the use of experimentation.

## Rectangle:

Construct rectangles with sides that are straight and parallel and angles that are right. Adjust the ratios to fit the needs of each individual object.

# Creating depth and dimension through shading:

## The play of light and shadow:

Be aware of how light interacts with the various items. Pay attention to the direction the light is coming from and how it is affecting the shadows. Utilizing this information, you will be able to give your designs more depth and dimension.

## Value scale:

Make it a habit to use your drawing tools to practice constructing a value scale that extends from light to dark. Your artwork will benefit from this since it will help you establish adequate shading and contrast.

## Various approaches to shading:

Try your hand at a variety of various shading methods like hatching (lines that are parallel to one another), cross-hatching (lines that overlap one another), stippling (dots), and blending. You will be able to generate volume and texture with the help of these approaches.

## Volume

In contrast to flat items, three-dimensional objects provide the impression of having volume and, as a result, suggest depth.

Depending on the position of the light source, a three-dimensional object will have sections that are highlighted as well as areas that are in shadow.

## Size

The farther distant an object is, the smaller it seems when viewed from that location, as this is how the rules of perspective work.

When you draw the same thing in different sizes, the viewer is led to believe that the smaller objects are further away, which contributes to the creation of a sense of depth in the drawing.

## Overlapping

If a body is able to hide a portion of another body behind itself, the hidden body must be located at a greater distance.

## Position/Height

When the base of the object is moved higher up on the drawing surface, it gives the impression that the object is further away.

In most circumstances, the bottom parts of items that are closer to the viewer are situated lower on the drawing surface, while the top parts of objects that are closer have been drawn higher.

## Contrast & Details

As one moves further away from an object, the contrast between the dark and light portions and the number of details in the object become less distinct.

In other words, when sketching or painting, regions with great contrast come forward, whilst regions with less contrast retreat into the background.

# How to Give the Appearance That Your Drawing Has Depth

## Make your drawing more three-dimensional by using scale.

If you ask a child to draw an avenue of trees, there is a good possibility that they will draw the trees next to one another or even stacked on top of one another. Why? This is due to the fact that they are drawing what they know rather than what they actually see, which is because they are aware that all of the trees are the same size.

If you take two trees that are exactly the same and place one of them further away from the other, the tree that is further away will appear to be smaller. It is clear that they are not of the same dimensions.

## Develop a sense of perspective in your drawing

Exaggerating tonal disparities is one tactic artists use to exert influence over viewers by utilizing their knowledge of light intensity.

It is possible for the artist to take two objects with nearly identical tones and intentionally distinguish between them by having one of the objects appear significantly lighter than the other. When compared to the other object, the darker one stands out and travels forward.

## Develop a sense of depth in the drawing (or painting) you are working on

When doing a monochrome drawing, the tonal range is easy to understand, but when painting, things aren't quite that plain and dry.

In the far distance, colors typically get more muted and fade away, but this is not always the case. When there is no haze in the atmosphere and the air is perfectly transparent, the colors of the things in the backdrop can appear to be startlingly vibrant. Here is where the distinction between warm and cold hues comes into play.

The warm colors, such as reds, oranges, and yellows, are the ones that are most striking to the eye and appear to advance further. The bluish-greens, blues, and purples become less prominent as the scene progresses.

## Applying Perspective to Your Drawing in Order to Create Depth

Even though we are aware that sizes get smaller as distance increases, the only way for them to look genuine is if the linear perspective is applied correctly.

There are a lot of artists who get their perspective all wrong. A line that extends into the distance must have a point that acts as its focal or vanishing point. If you are drawing a structure, it should be very simple. Your eye line will be aligned with the horizon, and the angles of the building will converge to point along the line.

When viewed from an acute angle, the building will appear to have two vanishing points, one on either side of the structure. If you are looking down from above, there are three.

When sketching a human or an animal, determining the location of the vanishing point can be significantly more challenging than when drawing other types of objects because the criteria remain the same.

# Drawing basic three-dimensional forms:

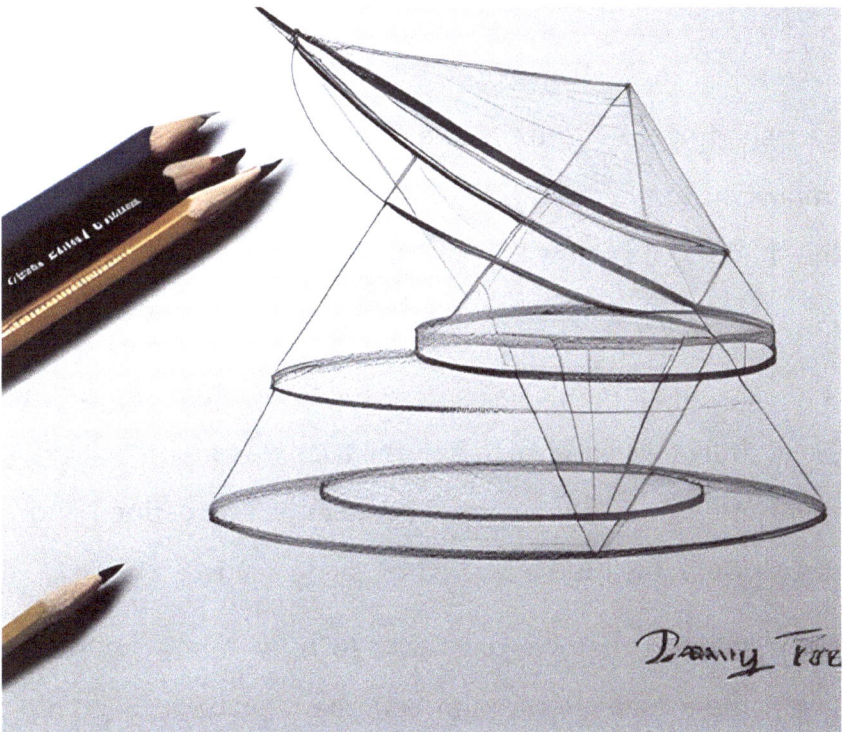

## Sphere:

To begin, draw a circle, and then shade it to give the impression that the circle has depth and is circular. Pay close attention to the way that its form is defined by the lighting and shadows.

## Cube:

You should begin by creating a square, and then you should draw other squares to build the sides of the object. To create the impression that it is three-dimensional, shade the sides in the appropriate manner.

## Cylinder:

Create a rough sketch of a cylinder, and then add details and shading to communicate the form of the object. It is important to pay attention to the curving surface as well as the shadows it creates.

## Cone:

First, create a triangle to serve as the foundation of the cone. Next, draw curved lines to link the triangle's points to form a point at the top of the cone. The form can be defined and a sense of volume can be created by using shade.

Keep in mind that the only way to fully comprehend and grasp these ideas is through consistent practice. Beginning with relatively straightforward topics, progressively work your way up to more involved topics. Your ability to show three-dimensional forms in your drawings in a convincing manner will improve as you practice watching, evaluating, and putting into practice these ideas.

# Developing Observation Skills

The cultivation of acute powers of observation is necessary for the success of any artist. The following are some suggestions that will assist you in developing your powers of observation:

## Understanding the concept of proportion:

Within a composition, proportion refers to the size and scale connections that exist between the various pieces that make up the whole. Train your eye to effectively estimate proportions by comparing the sizes and placements of a variety of objects or features. This will help you to develop your visual perception skills.

### Use comparable measuring techniques:

Keep your pencil or brush at arm's length, line it up with one feature, and evaluate how it compares to the others in terms of size and position.

**Pay attention to the space that is not being used:**

Take note of the contours and the gaps that exist between items or characteristics. These empty gaps can assist you in making more accurate determinations regarding proportions.

## Practicing with still life compositions:

- Create a still life with commonplace items by setting them up in an arrangement. Pick out things that vary in size, shape, and texture as much as possible.

- Concentrate on noticing and precisely expressing the relationships between items, as well as their dimensions and the way light and shadow play a role in the scene.

- When you feel ready, progressively work up to more difficult pieces, but get your feet wet with simpler ones first.

## Observing and drawing from nature:

- Spend some time outside, preferably in a natural setting such as a park, garden, or the countryside. Keep a sharp eye out and observe the natural world that surrounds you.

- It is important to pay attention to the myriad of minute details, as well as the textures, colors, and the way light interacts with the surroundings.
- Drawing natural subjects, such as trees, flowers, rocks, and landscapes, should be a part of your drawing routine. Pay close attention to the one-of-a-kind shapes and dimensions that each component possesses.

# Capturing facial features and expressions:

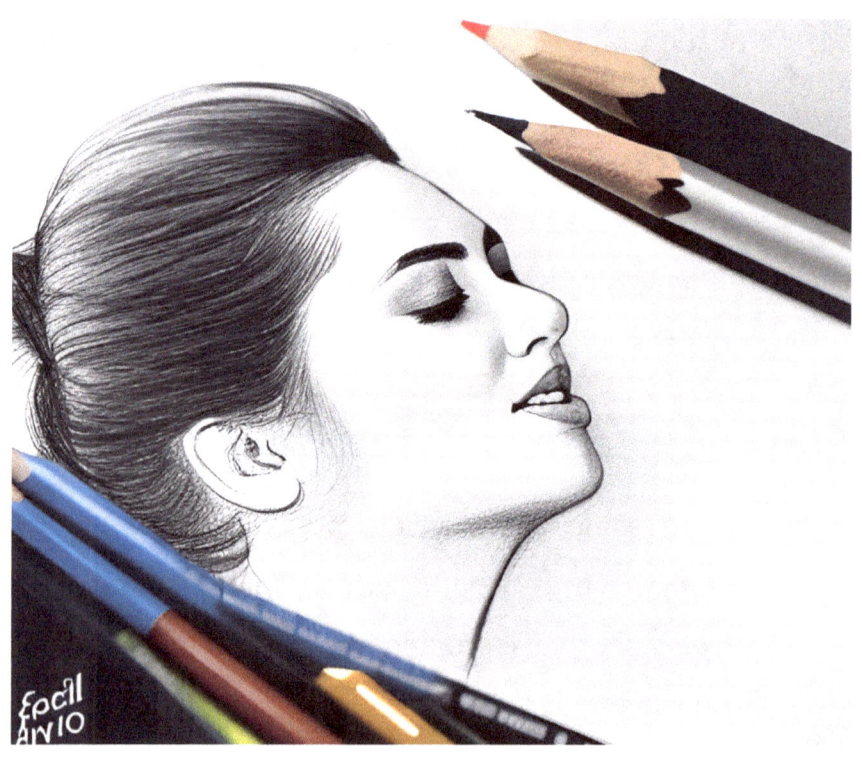

- Get yourself acquainted with the proportions and relationships of the various facial features, such as the eyes, the nose, the mouth, and the ears.

- Examine the faces of other people in a variety of lighting conditions and from a number of different angles to gain an understanding of how these aspects influence the look of facial features.

- Pay close attention to the nuances of expressions, such as the creases in the skin, the movements of the muscles, and the way the features of the face are positioned.

- Improving your ability to capture a subject's resemblance and expression can be accomplished by regularly drawing or sketching portraits, either from life or from images.

Always keep in mind the importance of having patience with yourself, and consider observation an ongoing activity. Your abilities will improve proportionally to the amount of time you spend actively observing the world around you. Your ability to convert what you see onto paper or canvas will significantly improve if you practice on a consistent basis and are willing to research and evaluate what you observe.

# Mastering Perspective Drawing

Learning how to draw in perspective is one of the most important skills you can have if you want your architectural drawings, landscapes, and cityscapes to look real and believable. Here's an overview to help you get started:

## Introduction to one-point and two-point perspective:

### Perspective that is Linear

The most common and well-known sort of viewpoint is called the linear perspective. Draw the objects in your scene so that as they get further away, they get smaller and smaller until they vanish at the "vanishing point."

Vanishing points are present in linear perspective, and the rest of the drawing is constructed on the basis of the lines that lead to those vanishing points.

### Eye Level

As you continue to educate yourself on perspective, you will likely come across the term "eye level" quite frequently. The height of the horizon is referred to as eye level in painting. In photography, it functions similarly to a line that indicates the height of the camera. The placement of the eye level contributes to the determination of the overall structure of your illustration.

For instance, if you configure the camera such that its eye level is the same as the character's eye level, the camera will gaze directly at the person.

## Horizontal and Vertical Eye Levels

Keep in mind the link between the eye level and the horizon as well. This is another important consideration.

If the camera is gazing in the same direction as the subject, the eye-level and the horizon will be at the same level.

When the eye level is raised, the horizon line will also move up to the new position. As a consequence of this, the position of the horizon will shift downwards as the eye level is lowered.

## One-point perspective:

In a perspective known as one-point, all lines meet at a single vanishing point, which is located on the horizon line. This method works particularly well for depicting things or scenes that are oriented so that they either face the viewer or turn their backs on them.

### Two different points of view:

In two-point perspective, lines of a scene converge on the horizon line at two distinct places known as vanishing points. This method is helpful for drawing objects or sceneries that have an angle or a corner that faces the viewer.

### Perspective from Three Different Angles

In three-point perspective, there are three points in the scene that are considered to be the vanishing point.

When using the two-point perspective approach, you can make the camera look up or look down at an object by adding a third vanishing point above (or below) the vanishing point that defines the two-point perspective.

When you draw from these angles, a type of distortion

Known as "height distortion" is created. This type of height distortion can be drawn using a technique called three-point perspective.

## Drawing basic architectural elements:

### Begin with the simplest of shapes:

To begin the process of constructing buildings or architectural features, begin by drawing simple geometric forms such as cubes, rectangles, and cylinders. This will serve as the framework for your design.

### Establish the line of the horizon:

Determine the level that your eye is looking at, then draw a line horizontally across your paper. This line is used to indicate the eye level of the observer and functions as the horizon line for perspective.

### Points of dissipation:

Depending on the sort of perspective you are employing, place the vanishing points on the horizon line. These are the spots that will be reached by every line that is parallel to every other line.

### Mark the construction lines as follows:

Create the framework of your items by drawing construction lines that originate from the vanishing points. These lines will be used to define where elements should be placed, as well as their sizes and proportions.

# Creating depth in landscapes and cityscapes:

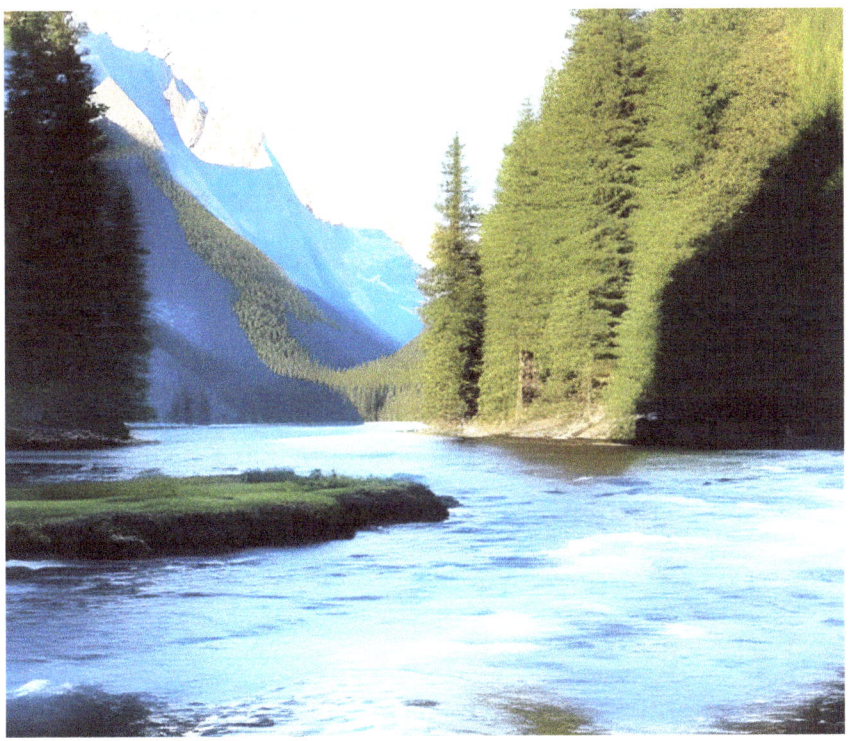

## Make use of overlapping:

Objects that overlap one another give the impression of depth and distance. Arrange the objects such that those that are further away are in the background and those that are closer to the spectator are in the foreground.

## Dimensions:

Objects that are nearer to the viewer appear larger, whilst objects that are further away appear more diminutive to the viewer. Applying this idea to your drawings will help you achieve a sense of depth as well as distance.

## Atmospheric perspective

Due to the influences of the atmosphere, objects in the distance appear to have less detail, a lighter value, and a bluish hue. This is referred to as an atmospheric perspective. In order to express this impact, lighter values and cooler colors should be used.

## Details and textures:

Objects that are closer to the spectator have a tendency to have more apparent details and textures, whereas objects that are further away appear smoother and have fewer details.

Keep in mind that the key to becoming an expert perspective drawer is to practice. Begin with straightforward items, then work your way up to more involved settings as you go. Researching various photographs, architectural plans, and reference images can help you gain a better grasp of perspective. You will develop self-assurance in your ability to create depth and realism in your architectural drawings, landscapes, and cityscapes with the passage of time and continued practice.

# Portraying Light and Shadow

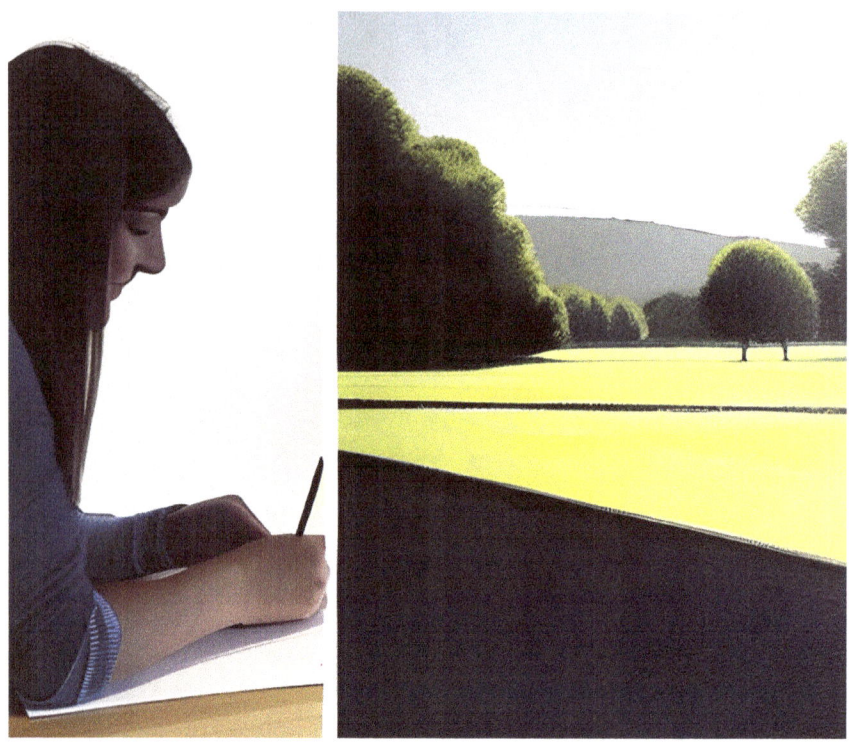

The ability to realistically portray light and shadow in your drawings can lend your artwork a sense of depth, atmosphere, and realism. The following is a guide that will help you understand how to effectively portray light and shadow:

## Understanding the behavior of light:

### The source of light:

Determine the path that the light is coming from and the kind of light that is present in the scene. It might be natural light, such as sunshine or the light of the moon, or it could be artificial light, such as from a lamp or candle.

### Magnitude of the light:

Take note of the way the light's intensity changes depending on how far away you are from its source. The light that falls on objects that are closer to the light source is stronger than the light that falls on objects that are further away.

### The nature of the light:

It is important to pay attention to whether the source of light is diffuse or direct because this determines whether the shadows are hazy or crisp and the overall atmosphere of the picture.

# Rendering basic light and shadow patterns:

### Highlight:

The part of an object that is the brightest because light is striking it directly. It frequently manifests as a little, luminous dot.

### Midtown:

The spectrum of tonal values that can be found between the highlight and the shadow. It is a representation of the object's primary color as well as its value.

### Shadow:

The region that does not receive any light coming in from outside. The nature of the light source as well as the shape of the item cast a shadow will determine both its intensity and its shape.

### Cast shadow:

The impression that something makes on its surroundings when it casts a shadow. Keep in mind that the angle of the light source and the distance between it and the object casting the shadow both have an effect on the form and the length of the shadow.

## Capturing different light sources and their effects:

### Natural light sources:

Throughout the course of the day, the sun's ray's move in different directions, which results in different shadows being cast and changing color temperatures being produced. Pay attention to how these changes occur. Take special note of the warm golden tones that are present at sunrise and sunset, as well as the cool blue tones that are present in the middle of the day or in areas that are shaded.

## Artificial light

Try out several different types of artificial lighting, like incandescent, fluorescent, or even candlelight, and see what you come up with. Light emanating from man-made sources. Take note of how the various light sources affect not just the color temperature but also the intensity of the light and the darkness of the shadows.

## Light that reflects off surfaces:

Pay close attention to the ways in which this kind of light influences the items that are located in the immediate area. The utilization of reflected light can soften the appearance of shadows while also bringing in additional light and color to an image.

Always be sure to complete the necessary study and examine the light and shadow in both the reference images and the actual situations. To achieve the appearance of realistic light and shadow in your drawings, try out a number of rendering techniques, such as hatching, cross-hatching, or blending, and see what results you get. You should engage in persistent practice and pay special attention to the dynamic between the light and the shadows in your drawings if you want to further develop your talents. Practicing on a regular basis will help you improve your skills.

## Methods of Shading for the Drawing Process

There is a wide variety of approaches that can be taken when applying shading to an object. The drawing will end up having a distinct texture and "feel" depending on the approach used. It's possible that the shading technique employed in the artwork will be determined by the media that was used to draw with.

The following are the most frequently used application techniques:

Hatching is the process of drawing lines in the same direction repeatedly. The creation of darker values requires drawing lines that are brought closer together. Increasing the amount of white space between the lines will result in values that are lighter. When dealing with spherical objects, the lines may somewhat curl around the shape, following the curves of the item.

## The use of hatching to create shading

The lines intersect and cross over one another to form a crosshatch pattern. The value that is created is determined by the density at which the lines pass over and intersect with each other.

## The use of cross hatching to create shading

Adjusting the amount of pressure that is applied to the medium or making use of a blending tool like a blending stump are both viable options for producing smooth gradations of value throughout the blending process.

## Blending

Rendering refers to the process of producing lighter values by removing the medium with an eraser. Blending is often done in combination with the application of this technique.

## Rendering

Lines that are drawn at random, with haphazard applications of crossing lines. The value that is created is determined by the frequency with which the lines cross over each other.

## Random lines

Stippling refers to the process of applying a large number of very small dots to a drawing in order to build up darker values. The value that is created is determined on the density of the dots.

## The Deception of Brightness

It is very simple to become preoccupied with the method by which the material is applied and to lose track of the purpose for why shading is being done in the first place.

After all, light is what allows us to see, and shading gives us information about the light within a scene. By analyzing the scene in terms of value and contrast, we are able to comprehend the light that is present.

## Value and contrast

The degree to which a color leans toward blackness or lightness is referred to as its value. When describing light values, one would use a tint, while when describing dark values, one would use a shade.

The idea of contrast places an emphasis on contrasts, or disparities. The presence of any form of difference between components, whether it be a difference in texture, color, size, or value, results in the creation of contrast. This can be the case regardless of the nature of the differences. It may be very subtle, or it could be very obvious. When it comes to shading, the first challenge that we have to take into consideration is the contrast that is produced by the differences in value.

A spectrum of values that are in opposition to one another is produced whenever light is shone on a subject. The intensity of the light has an effect on the degree of differentiation that may be seen between the values. When the light is going to be greater, the contrast is generally going to be higher than when it is going to be lower.

# The direction in which the light is coming from

On the subject, values are organized in a hierarchy that takes into account the position and magnitude of the light source (or sources). Let's look at what happens when there is just one light source shining on a smooth surface so that we may get a better understanding of how light acts on a subject and the things that are around it.

## Names of the places where shadows are cast

The viewer is informed about the placement of light on the subject as well as how the light interacts with the subject by the locations of each area of value on the subject. The way in which light behaves (or the way in which it is reflected) on the subject provides information on the texture and form of the object.

## Places of Economic Significance:

The highlight is the area of the topic at which the reflection of light is the brightest; it is also known as the focal point. In most cases, highlights are denoted by a very light value of the color, or in certain instances, by the color white.

## Mid Tone

The portions of the subject that are struck by light, but in a manner that is not as powerful as the highlight is referred to as the mid tones. In many instances, the real color (local color) or value of the topic is reflected in the subject's mid tone.

## Core shadow

The term "core shadow" refers to the region of the subject that is obscured from view by an obstruction that prevents light from reaching there and casting a shadow there. Core shadows are often represented by colors with darker tones than the surrounding area.

## Cast shadow

Shadows that are cast are areas of surrounding objects or surfaces that take on a darker value as a result of the casting of a shadow. Because of something else, light is prevented from entering these locations in their whole because a significant portion of it is being reflected away.

A portion of the light is reflected back onto the camera by the surfaces and objects in the surrounding area. This causes the light to reflect off of the items, producing a region with a lighter value.

## How to Give Shapes Shadows

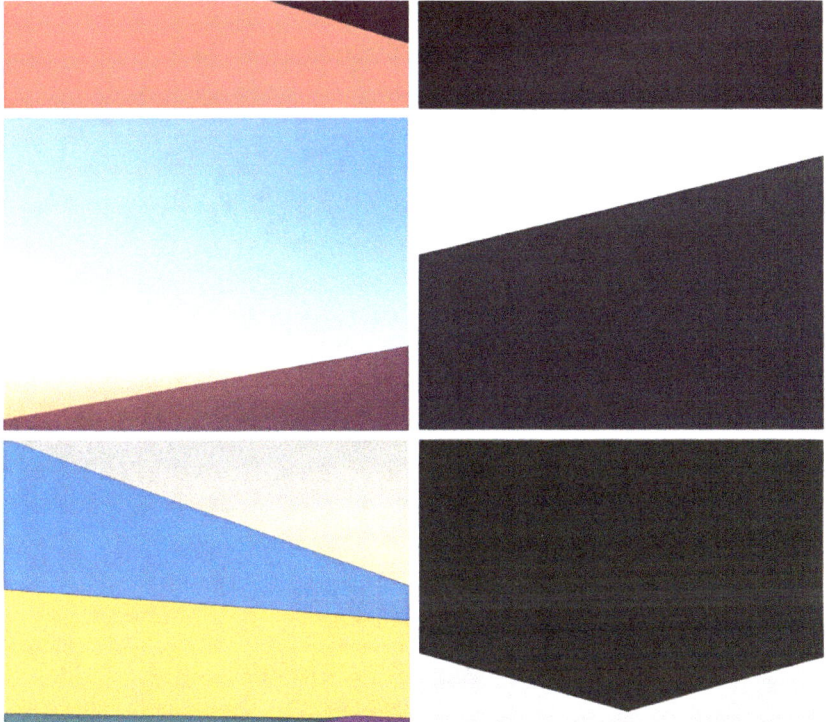

As was just said, shading also provides the viewer with information regarding the form of the object. When dealing with spheres, there is a progressive change in value (known as gradation). Depending on the intensity of the light, the value will either get darker or lighter. The same may be said for other curvy shapes like cones and cylinders.

In the case of geometric shapes with flat sides, such as a cube, the value tends to remain very stable across all faces, with only minor variations. There could be a different value on each face of the cube, signifying either the highlight, the middle tone, or the core shade.

But what about things that aren't cubes but have flat sides or planes instead of corners?

## How to Give Shadows to Forms That Are Hollow

A great number of things are either hollow or have recessed areas. In order to solve things like these, all we need to do is analyze the direction that light is coming from and think of it as a line.

If light is originating from a particular direction, then it should keep traveling in that direction until it strikes something. If the object is hollow, then the light will enter into the recess, forming a region of lighter value inside of it. On the other side of the edge of the recess, which is the side that is closest to the light source, shadows are generated.

## Maintaining Command of the Medium

Controlling the value that is produced by the shading that you apply is of the utmost significance, and this is true regardless of the medium that you use. The good news is that all you need is some patience and practice in order to gain control of the medium.

You are "half-way" there once you have a firm understanding of how light behaves and how you can transmit that behavior to the observer.

Drawing practice: a sphere, a cube, and a pyramid. Practice drawing these three basic forms. They should be shaded so as to provide the idea of a single light source employing a wide range of value. (To draw comparisons, you can use contrast as a tool).

# Adding Texture and Detail

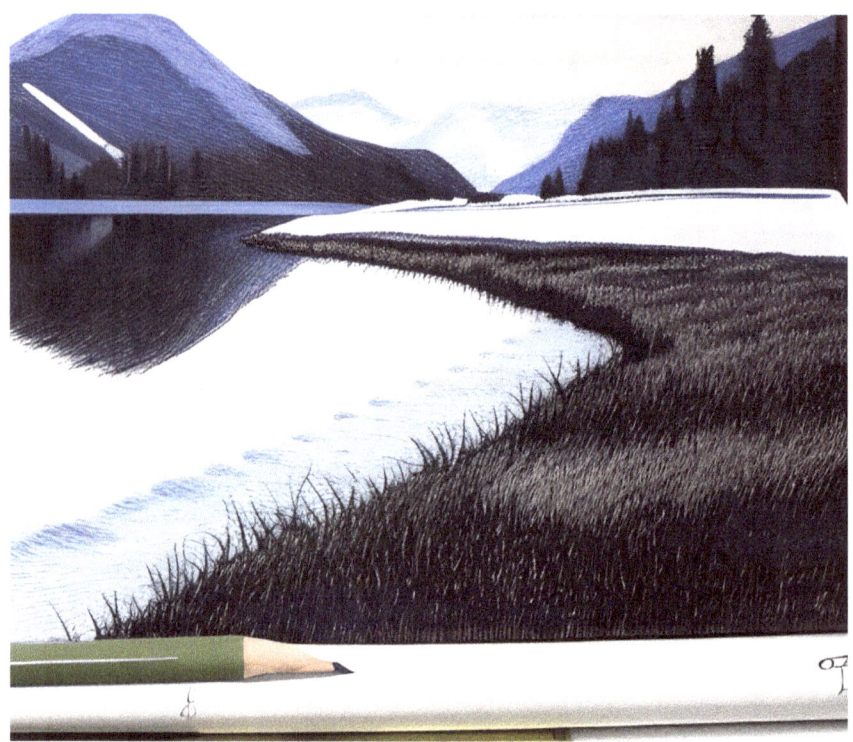

Bringing your drawings to life and making them more interesting to look at can be accomplished by giving them texture and detail. The following are some pointers that will assist you in successfully incorporating texture and detail:

## Using a wide variety of drawing methods to create a variety of textures:

Try out a variety of approaches to generating marks: in addition to utilizing a variety of strokes, experiment with a variety of tools and approaches to produce a variety of textures. For instance, you can use a method known as stippling to create a texture that resembles dots, or you can use a technique known as stumbling to create a texture that is rough and uneven.

## Examine and evaluate the following textures:

Spend some time looking at real-life textures as well as reference pictures. Pay close attention to the different forms, patterns, and particulars that may be found in each texture. For instance, when sketching fabric, examine how the folds and creases create particular textures, and when drawing greenery, notice the difference in leaf shapes and sizes. Another example would be to draw a person's face and study how their features change as they age.

## Get some practice imitating different textures:

To begin, take a separate sheet of paper and practice drawing a variety of various textures on it. Your focus should be on capturing the distinctive qualities of each texture. You may try drawing the roughness of a stone wall, the smoothness of glass, or the texture of tree bark. Pay close attention to the orientation of the lines, the placement of the dots, and the assortment of shape variations that are contained inside each texture.

# Developing convincing surface textures through the use of shading and hatching:

## Observe surface textures:

Pay attention to the ways in which light interacts with different surfaces to produce highlights and shadows. For instance, the surface of a glossy object will have highlights that are more prominent and shadows that are more distinct, but a matte surface will have transitions that are more subtle. For the purpose of conveying the form and depth of the texture, shading techniques such as hatching, cross-hatching, and stippling might be utilized.

## Change pressure and the density

By altering the pressure and density with which you apply your strokes, you may create sections that are lighter or darker, as well as variations in texture and value. For instance, while sketching a rough texture, you can use strokes that are heavier and more irregular in order to portray the roughness of the texture. On the other hand, if you want to create the impression of a smooth texture, you should try to use lighter and smoother strokes. This will provide the impression of a softer appearance.

# Incorporating details with the goal of improving the drawing as a whole:

## Make use of reference photos:

Reference images are a rich source of knowledge as well as inspiration when it comes to adding details to your designs. When working on a particular topic, it is helpful to compile a collection of reference photographs that illustrate the minute nuances you wish to portray. Pay close attention to the subject matter, specifically the small lines, textures, and patterns that are there.

## Focus on key details:

Your drawing needs not have the same amount of detail in every single element of it. Find the focus points or regions of interest in your piece, and pay more attention to and be more precise with those places. These carefully chosen details will assist direct the attention of the spectator and create an impactful image.

# Make use of a variety of drawing tools, including:

You should experiment with a wide range of sketching tools to achieve the amount of detail you intend to achieve in your drawings. When you are taking notes of specific information, you should consider using a pen or pencil that has a very fine tip. Additionally, erasers or blending stumps can be used to alter textures or make subtle transitions, particularly in areas that require smoother gradients or softer textures. This is particularly useful in the context of the previous sentence. When working in fields such as these, this is a really helpful skill to have.

You can effectively improve the visual appeal and realism of your drawings by experimenting with a variety of mark-making procedures, conducting study on textures, developing your skills in observation, and adding a suitable level of detail to your drawings. Always keep in mind how important it is to explore, to keep up a constant practice regimen, and to pay great attention to the unique aspects of each and every detail and texture that you try to imitate.

## Drawing Texture: Some Helpful Hints

The following are some pointers and suggestions for incorporating texture into your drawings:

- Make use of a wide array of different methods for making marks. This could involve stippling, scribbling, hatching, or cross hatching.

- When producing marks, apply it with varying amounts of pressure. Marks that are easier to make will result in a smoother texture, while marks that are tougher to make will result in a more defined texture.

- Make use of a wide range of tools. Pens and charcoal are two other tools that can be used to generate texture in addition to pencils.

- Layer your marks. As a result, an effect that is richer in texture will be produced as a result of the interaction between the various layers of marks.

- Take into consideration the direction that your marks are going. This may have a significant bearing on the overall texture of the finished product. By adjusting the curve, direction, and sharpness of the marks, you may give the impression that they were created organically.

- Consider the depth of the texture you want to create. This is particularly crucial when generating texture using hatching or cross hatching because thinner lines will provide a distinct impact than broader lines would.

- Make use of a variety of values. Your texture will have more depth and dimension as a result of this.
- Experiment! Experiment with a variety of methods for generating marks and observe the impact that each one has on the texture you create.

# Conclusion

In conclusion, drawing is an extremely enjoyable and satisfying artistic hobby that provides a great deal of joy and contentment. It gives you the opportunity to express yourself emotionally, tap into your creative potential, and discover the world around you in a way that is singular to you. Throughout this tutorial, we have looked into a variety of ideas and procedures that are essential to developing your skills as an artist.

You can make a safe haven for your artistic activities by preparing the appropriate supplies and setting up a workplace that is exclusively for that purpose. You will have the liberty and convenience to totally submerge yourself in the creative process when you have access to a space that is well-appointed. You will have more freedom to experiment and investigate a wide range of drawing methods and styles if you are equipped with a selection of drawing surfaces, as well as a number of different pencils, pens, and brushes to choose from.

Learning to sketch in perspective is the first step toward developing a sense of depth and dimension in your artwork. Your ability to accurately represent architectural features is enhanced by your knowledge of one-point and two-point perspective, which in turn gives your drawings a sense of realism and the believability of space. You may create a convincing illusion of depth by applying the concepts of perspective into your landscapes and cityscapes. This will allow you to capture the expansiveness and grandeur of the world that surrounds you.

The way in which light behaves and how it engages with objects is one of the most fundamental aspects of sketching. You can efficiently portray fundamental light and shadow patterns if you pay attention to how light illuminates and casts shadows on a surface. You are able to portray the atmosphere and mood of your sceneries more accurately if you have a good understanding of the many aspects of light sources, such as the qualities of natural sunlight, artificial interior lighting, and the soft glow of a candle. Your drawings will appear more three-dimensional, realistic, and full of volume if you make strategic use of highlights, shadows, and midtowns.

Bringing your drawings to life and making them more visually appealing and immersive can be accomplished by adding texture and depth. You can create a broad variety of textures that accurately depict diverse surfaces by experimenting with a variety of techniques, such as cross-hatching, stippling, or blending. These textures can range from the abrasiveness of tree bark to the velvety smoothness of a flower petal. You can create realistic textures by utilizing shading and hatching techniques, which put an emphasis on the way light and shadow interact with the elements in your drawing. The entire drawing is improved by the incorporation of fine details, which adds depth, character, and visual interest to the piece.

Drawing is a voyage of continual learning and improvement, so keep that in mind as you continue to discover new artistic techniques and expand your artistic abilities. Do not be afraid to take risks and test the limits of your capabilities; instead, view obstacles as opportunities for personal growth and embrace them as such. Try your hand at a variety of artistic approaches, topics, and mediums, and let your natural inquisitiveness direct you. Embrace the pleasure of creation as each new mark you make with your pen or brush puts you that much closer to bringing your artistic vision to life.

Drawing is not only a form of artistic expression, but it is also a way to find personal fulfillment and connect with others.

www.ingramcontent.com/pod-product-compliance
Lightning Source LLC
Chambersburg PA
CBHW062243290526
45794CB00006B/2381